THE 12 WORST SHIPWRECKS OF ALL TIME

by Joan Axelrod-Contrada

12 STORY LIBRARY

www.12StoryLibrary.com

12-Story Library is an imprint of Bookstaves.

Photographs ©: NOAA/Institute for Exploration/University of Rhode Island, cover, 1; jjsala/CC2.0, 4; Steven Senne/Associated Press, 5; INTERFOTO/Alamy Stock Photo, 6; Library of Congress, 7; PD, 8; Library of Congress, 9; Thomas W. Bankes/PD, 10; Library of Congress, 11; lindsaybridge/CC2.0, 12; Willie Salenga/Associated Press, 13; Childs, J/PD, 14; EFE News Agency/Alamy Stock Photo, 15; PD, 16; W.G. MacLaughlan. Canada. Canadian Intellectual Property Office. Library and Archives Canada, C-017501/CC2.0, 17; GL Archive/Alamy Stock Photo, 18; Library of Congress, 19; mauritius images GmbH/Alamy Stock Photo, 20; Augst/CC3.0, 21; PD, 22; Library of Congress, 23; Rob Stapleton/Associated Press, 24; PH2 POCHE/US Navy, 25; US Navy, 26; Ggia/CC4.0, 27; AnEduard/Shutterstock.com, 28; Chayantorn Tongmorn/Shutterstock.com, 29

ISBN
978-1-63235-540-9 (hardcover)
978-1-63235-605-5 (paperback)
978-1-63235-659-8 (ebook)

Library of Congress Control Number: 2018947110

Printed in the United States of America
Mankato, MN
June 2018

About the Cover

The bow of the *Titanic*, photographed in 2004.

Table of Contents

1

Pirate Ship *Whydah Gally* Sunk by Atlantic Storm

It was 1717. Pirate captain Samuel "Black Sam" Bellamy sailed the seas in search of ships to rob. The captain called himself the Robin Hood of the Sea. He stole from rich merchants. He then shared the booty with his pirates.

The ship's bell from the *Whydah Gally*, is in the Houston Museum of Natural Science.

Bellamy's crew included people who had once been enslaved. Black sailors worked alongside white shipmates as equals. Bellamy was not a black man. He got his nickname "Black Sam" for his long, dark hair. He refused to powder it, like other captains did.

In February 1717, Black Sam spotted a ship on the Caribbean Sea. He thought it could be perfect for his pirate fleet. The ship was huge. It was also very fast. Bellamy decided to go after it.

The ship Black Sam chased was the *Whydah Gally*. It was a slave ship. After three days, Bellamy captured the *Whydah Gally*. He took over the

Gold coins discovered off the coast of New England, where the *Whydah Gally* sank.

treasure-filled vessel and steered toward New England.

Black Sam's good fortune would run out. In April 1717, a fierce Atlantic storm sank the *Whydah Gally.* Millions in gold, ivory, and goods fell to the ocean floor. Bellamy and all but two crew members died.

THINK ABOUT IT

Many pirates started off working on merchant ships. As seamen, they were often treated badly. Would you become a pirate if you thought you'd be treated better than a regular seaman?

$139 million

Black Sam Bellamy's riches in 2018 dollars.

- Black Sam called himself the Robin Hood of the Sea.
- The pirate captain captured the slave ship *Whydah Gally.*
- A powerful storm sank the ship in April 1717.

2

Giant Whale Rams, Sinks Whaleship *Essex*

A 19th-century wood engraving of the whale attack.

On November 20, 1820, a giant sperm whale smashed into the whaleship *Essex*. The impact tore a hole in the ship. Water gushed in. The whale rammed the ship a second time. The *Essex* capsized.

Crew members had set sail from Nantucket in the US State of Massachusetts. Nantucket and nearby New Bedford were favored ports for sperm whale hunting. Hundreds of ships left each year. Whale blubber and oil were brought back for use in candles and other goods.

After the *Essex* capsized, 20 crew members escaped onto three small boats. They were thousands of miles from land. They lay under the blazing sun. Before long, they ran out of

85

Length in feet (26 m) of the sperm whale that attacked the whaleship *Essex*.

- The ship sank after the whale rammed it a second time.
- Five crew members were rescued after living for months on small boats.
- The shipwreck inspired the famous novel *Moby Dick*.

WHY WOULD A WHALE ATTACK A SHIP?

Whales rarely go after ships. However, it happens. Scientists wonder why. There are at least two theories. One theory says whales remember being harpooned or seeing their young attacked. The other says whales think hammering sounds from a ship are the clicks of rival males. Whales might strike in anger or self-defense.

food. They turned to cannibalism to survive.

After months at sea, seamen on two of the boats were saved by passing ships. In all, five sailors survived. One crew member wrote a book about the sinking. His tale inspired Herman Melville to write the famous novel *Moby Dick*.

A 1954 model of the whaleship *Essex*.

3 "Unsinkable" *Titanic* Goes Down After Hitting Iceberg

On a spring day in 1912, passengers in fur coats and gold cufflinks boarded a ship. Its nickname was the Millionaire's Special. It was the *Titanic*, the largest, most modern ship ever built. Many people believed it was unsinkable.

The *Titanic* departed Southampton, England, on April 10, 1912. Its destination was New York City. As the ship crossed the Atlantic, people aboard would enjoy elegant dinners and fancy balls.

But on the fourth day of the trip, the *Titanic* ignored ice warnings from other ships. When a lookout spotted an iceberg, it was too late. The ship swerved to avoid hitting it head-on. But the iceberg grazed the ship's side. The *Titanic* filled with seawater.

Titanic at the dock in Southampton on April 1, 1912.

Panic broke out. Passengers tried to get on lifeboats. But there was only enough room for one-third of those on board. Crewmen led first-class travelers to safety. Third-class travelers were trapped below decks.

Many dramas unfolded while the ship went down. Some passengers died rather than leave their loved ones. One man changed into formal evening dress. He wanted to die looking like a gentleman. About 1,500 passengers and crew members perished. At the time, it was the worst peacetime shipwreck in history.

The sinking of the *Titanic* inspired many books and movies. It also prompted new safety guidelines. Ships were required to carry enough lifeboats to hold all passengers.

THE NEW YORK HERALD.

THE TITANIC SINKS WITH 1,800 ON BOARD; ONLY 675, MOSTLY WOMEN AND CHILDREN, SAVED

MOST APPALLING DISASTER IN MARINE HISTORY OCCURS WHEN WORLD'S LARGEST STEAMSHIP STRIKES GIGANTIC ICEBERG AT NIGHT

Scores of World's Most Widely Known Persons, Including Colonel John Jacob Astor and His Wife, William T. Stead and Isidor Straus Among Those Whose Fate Is in Doubt.

J. Bruce Ismay, Head of the White Star Line; Mr. and Mrs. George D. Widener, the Countess of Rothes and Mrs. Henry B. Harris Are Some of Those Saved.

THINK ABOUT IT

Many people believed the *Titanic* was unsinkable. Do you think this influenced how the captain operated the ship? Why or why not?

2,240

Passengers and crew on the *Titanic.*

- The ship was traveling from England to the United States.
- Ice warnings from other ships were ignored.
- The catastrophe killed about 1,500 passengers and crew members.

4

Union Soldiers Perish in *Sultana* Shipwreck

This image from April 26, 1865, shows how overcrowded the steamship was.

The US Civil War had finally ended. On April 26, 1865, thousands of Union soldiers crowded aboard the steamship *Sultana*. All had been prisoners of war. They had just been released. The captain squeezed in six times the number of passengers legally allowed on his ship. He made more money that way. The ship would depart from Vicksburg, Mississippi.

Before leaving Vicksburg, one of the ship's boilers sprang a leak. A proper repair would take three or four days. The captain didn't want to wait. He ordered a quick fix. A patch was applied to the boiler.

The soldiers on the *Sultana* talked about their memories of the war. Fighting on the battlefield. Being captured. What it was like to be a prisoner of war. They were happy to be going home.

2,300

Number of Union soldiers onboard the *Sultana*.

- Union soldiers were being returned to the North after the US Civil War.
- The *Sultana* caught fire when three of its boilers exploded.
- Confederate locals helped save some Union soldiers, but casualties were high.

A CATASTROPHE GOES UNNOTICED

The story of the *Sultana* remained lost in history for years. The reason was the timing of when it happened. Many important stories were being told at the same time. The end of the Civil War was one. The assassination of President Abraham Lincoln on April 14 was another.

At 2:00 a.m. on April 27, three of the ship's four boilers exploded. Fire spread throughout the ship. Passengers and crew jumped into the river. The ship sank about seven miles north (11 km) of Memphis, Tennessee.

Just days earlier, locals had fought as Confederate soldiers against the Union army. Now some rushed to the aid of the northerners. Almost 800 people were saved. However, many more died. About 1,700 people lost their lives in the *Sultana* disaster.

An illustration of the catastrophe from *Harper's Weekly*.

5

Doña Paz Ferry Disaster an Asian *Titanic*

People in the Philippines often travel by ferry. The nation is made up of many islands. Going back and forth by water is simplest. The ferry system usually gets people where they need to go. But on the night of December 20, 1987, ferry travel turned disastrous.

On this night, a ferry called the *Doña Paz* crossed the sea south of the capital city of Manila. By 10:00 p.m., most travelers were asleep in their cabins. The captain of the ferry drank beer and watched TV. He left an inexperienced crew member to steer the ship. In the darkness, this person did not see another vessel approach. It was the oil tanker *Vector.*

The *Doña Paz* collided with the Vector. The tanker caught on fire. The fire spread to the *Doña Paz.* As the ferry burned, many people jumped overboard into waters full of

The *Doña Paz* ferry in 1984.

There were so many victims, funerals were held at Manila's Rizal Memorial Coliseum.

sharks. But sharks were not the only concern. Spilled oil was burning on the water.

More than 4,000 people died in the wreck. One reason it was so deadly is because there were too many people on board. Passengers had been sleeping four to a bed.

Only 24 passengers survived the accident. People nicknamed the shipwreck the Asian *Titanic*. It was the worst peacetime shipwreck in history.

$4,343

Amount each victim's heirs received in 2017, 30 years after the tragedy.

- Because the Philippines is a nation of islands, people often travel by ferry.
- A ferry named the *Doña Paz* collided with an oil tanker on December 20, 1987.
- Thousands perished in what became known as the Asian *Titanic*.

6

Hurricane Sinks "Ship of Gold"

The SS *Central America* left a port on the Panama Canal on September 3, 1857. It sailed under bright blue skies and calm winds. It was loaded with passengers and tons of gold. People who had gone west for the California Gold Rush were returning east with their riches. The *Central America* made a stop in Havana, Cuba, then went back to sea. Its destination was New York City. There was a fortune in gold onboard the ship.

On September 9, a breeze became a gale-force wind. The wind became a hurricane. By September 11, the sails were ripped to shreds. The ship sprang a leak. Then the boiler stopped working. There was no longer any way to control the ship. It was tossed around by the waves.

On September 12, two ships were sighted on the horizon. Women and children were put on lifeboats and rescued. Later that day, the *Central America* sank off the coast of the

Gold bullion from the *Central America*.

Carolinas. More than 420 people were killed. All the gold sank to the bottom of the sea. Ever since, the *Central America* has been called the "Ship of Gold."

TREASURE HUNTER DISCOVERS BURIED GOLD

Treasure hunter Thomas Thompson wanted to find the SS *Central America* and its gold. He borrowed millions of dollars and built a state-of-the-art robot. The robot, named Nemo, explored the ocean floor. In 1987, it found the missing gold. Thompson became famous. But he could not pay his debts. Instead, he went into hiding. Officials found him and put him in prison in 2015.

$54 million

Value of the ship's treasure in present-day dollars.

- The SS *Central America* carried passengers who got rich in the California Gold Rush.
- The ship sank off the coast of the Carolinas during a hurricane.
- More than 400 lives were lost, and tons of gold sank to the bottom of the ocean.

7 Ships Carrying War Cargo Collide in Canadian Harbor

Taken from about 1 mile (1.6 km) away, this is believed to be the only photograph of the explosion.

Two ships jockeyed for position in the early morning fog on December 6, 1917. They both tried to squeeze through the narrow Canadian harbor of Halifax.

The ships held supplies meant to help defeat Germany in World War I. The French ship *Mont-Blanc* carried munitions for the war. The Norwegian ship *Imo* held relief supplies. The *Mont-Blanc* was headed one way. The *Imo* was headed the other.

The captain of the *Mont-Blanc* blew his whistle in warning. He wanted the captain of the *Imo* to yield. The *Imo* captain, however, refused to wait. Around 8:45 a.m., the two ships collided. Sparks flew. Fuel spilled in the *Mont-Blanc* and the ship caught on fire. Its crew escaped on a lifeboat. But the blazing ship brushed against the dock. This led to the pier

9,000

People injured in the explosion at Halifax harbor.

- French and Norwegian ships collided in the Canadian port of Halifax in 1917.
- War munitions caught on fire, causing the *Mont-Blanc* to explode.
- The blast killed more than 1,800 people and blinded 200 others.

going up in flames. At 9:05 a.m., the *Mont-Blanc* exploded.

The force of the ship's explosion was enormous. Fragments of the *Mont-Blanc* crashed through buildings in Halifax. Splintering glass and flying debris blinded 200 people. More than 1,800 people were killed. The shock wave shattered windows 50 miles away (80 km). A huge, dark cloud rose over the city. After the accident, new rules were put in place to improve harbor safety.

Damage to Halifax buildings from the blast.

8 German Submarine Sinks Passenger Ship *Lusitania*

People called the *Lusitania* the Greyhound of the Seas. That's because the ship was so fast on the water. The *Lusitania* left New York City on May 1, 1915. It was bringing passengers to Liverpool, England.

Europe at the time was gripped by World War I. The United States was not yet involved in the war. Germany declared the waters around England fair game for warfare. But attacking a passenger ship would be a bold move. Besides, the *Lusitania* could speed away from danger. That's what people thought, anyway.

On the Atlantic, foggy weather hurt the ship's ability to travel quickly. The *Lusitania* slowed down as it approached the British Isles. The captain doubted Germany would act on its threat to target ships in British waters. So he steered straight into harm's way.

Soon after, a torpedo from a German submarine shook the *Lusitania*. The ship sank in 18 minutes. Of the

The *Lusitania* arriving in New York City in 1907.

An illustration of the fateful event from the *New York Herald*.

1,195 people who died, 128 were Americans.

Outrage grew in the United States. People were angry that Germany sank a ship carrying US citizens. The sinking of the *Lusitania* was a big reason why the United States entered World War I. The nation could no longer remain neutral.

1,959

Passengers onboard the *Lusitania*.

- The *Lusitania* was famous for its speed.
- The captain ignored wartime threats.
- The ship sank after being attacked by a German submarine.

MISTAKEN FOR DEAD

Nettie Moore escaped onto a lifeboat with her husband and infant son. But the lifeboat sank. Her husband and son drowned. Nettie herself was mistaken for dead. Then her brother saw her eyelids flutter. Nettie was alive! She went on to become a nurse midwife, delivering other people's babies.

9

Soviet Submarine Torpedoes Ship of Refugees

World War II was winding down in January 1945. The Soviet army was advancing on Poland. This put Germans in the area at risk. Germany sent a ship to bring refugees and military personnel home.

The *Wilhelm Gustloff* was chosen for the rescue mission. In its early years, the vessel had served as a cruise ship. Thousands of passengers loyal to the Nazi party had traveled in luxury aboard the *Gustloff.* But the ship had not been operated regularly in years. The captain worried the engines might fail. He decided to travel slowly to avoid putting too much strain on them.

A Soviet submarine fired three torpedoes at the ship. The *Gustloff* sank in about an hour. More than 9,000 people lost their lives. Many of the victims were women and children. Despite the massive loss of life, few people heard about the *Gustloff*. The news was barely reported. Germany wanted to keep its war losses secret.

Some people wondered if attacking a ship with so many women and children was a war crime. Allies fighting Germany in the war decided it was not. The reason was because the ship also carried weapons and soldiers. The sinking of the *Gustloff* is the deadliest shipwreck in history.

10,582

Number of passengers onboard the *Wilhelm Gustloff*. It was built to hold 1,900.

- Near the end of World War II, Germany sent a ship to Poland to rescue refugees.
- The *Gustloff* was torpedoed by a Soviet submarine.
- Few people learned of the tragedy because Germany kept it quiet.

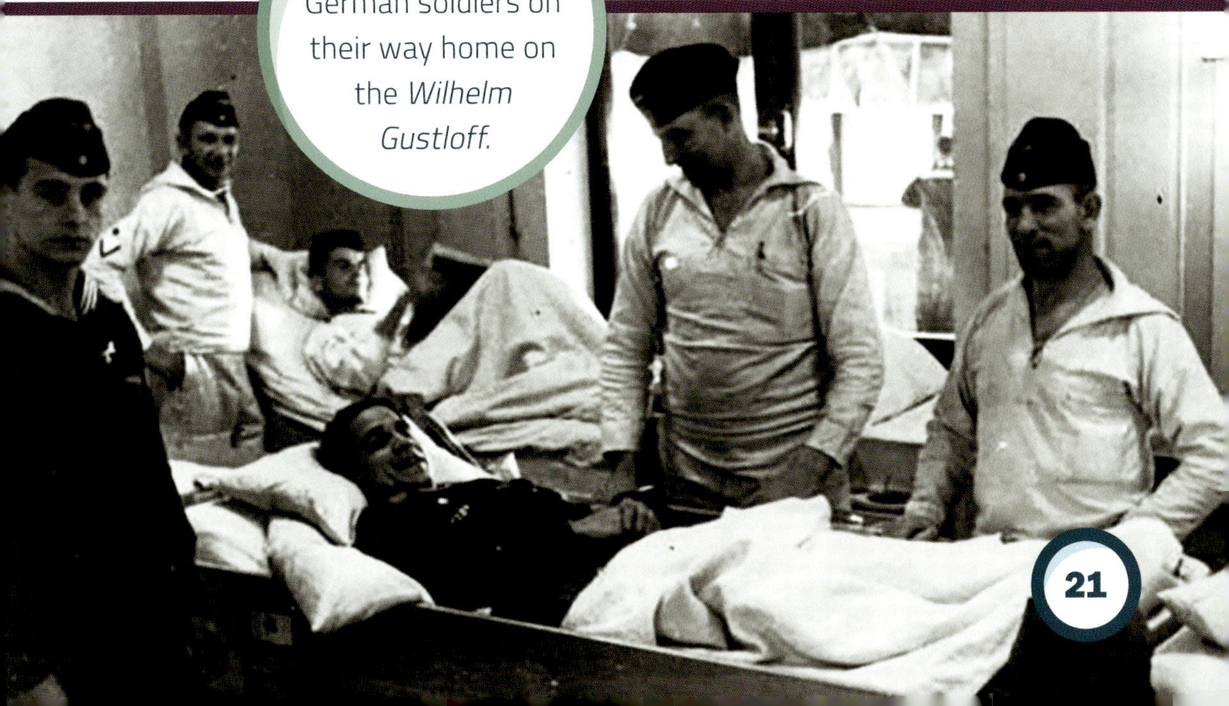

Wounded German soldiers on their way home on the *Wilhelm Gustloff*.

10

New York Picnic Outing Turns Deadly in Steamboat Fire

New-York Tribune.

PRICE THREE CENTS.

V^OL. LXIV....N^O. 21,032.

NEW-YORK, THURSDAY, JUNE 16, 1904.—SIXTEEN PAGES.

THE BURNING OF THE EXCURSION BOAT GENERAL SLOCUM.

BODIES ALONG THE BEACH AT NORTH BROTHER ISLAND.

CAPTAIN VAN SCHAICK.

THE SLOCUM AS SHE STARTED ON HER TRIP.

SEARCHING FOR BODIES IN THE WRECK OF THE SLOCUM.

HORROR IN EAST RIVER

THE SLOCUM AND OTHER DISASTERS.

Loss of Life by General Slocum Disaster, About 700; Injured and Missing.

THE CAPTAIN'S STORY.

THEORY AS TO THE ORIGIN

On June 15, 1904, members of a church group from New York City's Little Germany chatted excitedly. The group had plans to get out of the city. They would ride on a steamboat to Long Island for a church picnic.

The SS *General Slocum* sailed down the East River under sunny skies. It was a fine day. Passengers smelled chowder cooking below deck. They looked forward to their picnic.

At some point, smoke began to rise into the air. Then flames rose up onto the deck from below. The *General Slocum* was on fire.

The captain could have made a quick landing. Instead, he chose a rocky beach further away. Frantic men, women, and children plunged

All that was left of the *General Slocum* after being raised from the river.

into the water. The crew handed out life jackets. Many were rotten and fell apart.

More than 1,000 people died that day. A jury later found the captain guilty of negligence. The fire on the *General Slocum* was New York's worst disaster until the terrorist attacks of September 11, 2011.

HERO DROWNS AFTER SAVING PASSENGERS

Brave people plunged into the water to save others. They dragged struggling passengers to safety. Helping people put their own lives at risk. In fact, not all of the rescuers survived. One police officer rescued eleven passengers. When he tried to save a twelfth person, he drowned.

1,358

Number of people onboard the *General Slocum*.

- The *General Slocum* carried a church group from New York City on a picnic outing.
- A fire swept through the ship, forcing people to jump into the water.
- The captain failed to make a quick landing, which added to the death toll.

11

Exxon Valdez Disaster Covers Alaskan Coast in Oil

A smaller ship, the *Exxon Baton Rouge,* attempts to off-load crude from the *Exxon Valdez.*

1,300

Miles of coastline (2,092 km) damaged by the oil spill.

- The *Exxon Valdez* slammed into a reef on March 24, 1989.
- Oil spilled from the tanker, polluting the water and killing wildlife.
- People in fishing towns along the coast lost their way of life.

It was just after midnight on March 24, 1989. On Prince William Sound in Alaska, the dark sky blended into the sea. On the water, a huge oil tanker named the *Exxon Valdez* chugged down the sound. In a moment, an environmental catastrophe was unleashed.

The captain of the *Exxon Valdez* had been drinking alcohol that day. The oil tanker collided with a reef. The ship's hull ripped open on impact. Eleven million gallons of crude oil poured into Prince William Sound. Making matters worse, a huge storm blew in from the ocean. It helped spread the oil to the shoreline. The mess could not be contained.

Hundreds of thousands of seabirds, mammals, and fish died as a result of the oil spill. Wildlife workers cleaned oil off some of the creatures to save them. However, many animals could not be rescued. Oil also hurt animals up the food chain. Brown bears died after eating birds and fish covered in oil. Crude oil remains buried below the surface of Alaskan beaches to this day.

People in fishing towns along the Alaskan coast lost their way of life after the spill. They had to find new jobs. Lawmakers passed new laws to protect waters from oil spills.

Massive efforts were required to clean the shoreline.

12 Refugees and Migrants Make Dangerous Crossings

They come from poor and troubled lands. Some are fleeing war or persecution. Some are seeking better lives for themselves and their families. They crowd into boats with no names. Their vessels have no fancy cabins. There is no fine dining. Travelers are lucky if they have room to lie down. They just want to stay alive.

Hundreds of thousands of refugees and migrants are crossing the Mediterranean Sea on small, rickety boats. They are on their way to Europe. They want to escape hard lives in Africa and the Middle East.

Since 1993, more than 33,000 people have died trying to reach Europe. Experts believe this number is less than half the real number. The International Organization for Migration has called the Mediterranean Sea the deadliest border in the world.

Smugglers are a big part of the problem. They promise to help migrants and refugees get into Europe illegally. Migrants and

Rescue teams help refugees from an overcrowded boat.

refugees pay smugglers thousands of dollars for a place on broken-down boats. Once on board, there is a good chance they will not make it to land.

Crossing the sea in flimsy boats is very risky. The small boats easily overturn in the water. The passengers don't have enough food or water. Those who don't drown often die of starvation or dehydration. More people have died making this dangerous voyage than in any shipwreck in history.

3,100

Estimated number of migrants and refugees who died on the Mediterranean Sea in 2017.

- Refugees and migrants from the Middle East and Africa cross the Mediterranean Sea to Europe.
- They travel on flimsy boats, hoping to make new lives in Europe.
- Thousands die each year on the Mediterranean Sea.

THINK ABOUT IT

Do you believe all nations should let refugees in? How might this affect people who already live there? What challenges might the refugees face as newcomers?

Staying Safe If There Is a Shipwreck

- If you're planning an outing or a journey on a boat, pack a survival kit. Include a compass, flashlight, first aid kit, sunscreen, and knife. You might also include some fresh water and food rations, and a mirror for signaling for help.

- Wear a life vest at all times. Choose one that has been approved by federal officials where you live. Make sure it's in good condition.

- On a ship, know the exits closest to your cabin. Learn the escape routes for other areas of the ship where you spend time.

- Know where the lifeboats are located and which one you are assigned to.

- If you end up in a river, lake, or ocean without a life vest, you can make your clothes into flotation devices. Look online for articles and videos that tell you how to do this.
- Swim away from a sinking boat or ship. Moving away can help you to avoid being injured by the propeller.
- Use deep breathing to stay calm. Practice breathing techniques ahead of time.
- Keep your spirits up. If you find yourself on a lifeboat, try to stay upbeat by talking, singing, or playing games with other people.

Glossary

cannibalism
The act of eating one's own kind.

harpoon
A barbed spear for hunting whales.

lifeboat
A boat carried on a ship or kept on shore to rescue people at sea.

lookout
One who keeps watch for danger.

migrant
A person moving to a new place.

munitions
Military equipment and supply used for fighting.

negligence
Failure to use proper caution.

pirate
A person who attacks and robs ships at sea.

propeller
A device with two or more blades that turns quickly to power a boat or aircraft.

refugee
A person forced to flee his or her country.

slave ship
European ship carrying kidnapped Africans to be sold into slavery.

smuggler
Someone who takes goods or people out of a country illegally.

For More Information

Books

Mullenbach, Cheryl. *Torpedoed! A World War II Story of a Sinking Passenger Ship and Two Children's Survival at Sea.* Chicago, IL: Chicago Review Press, 2017.

Otfinoski, Steven. *Smooth Sea and a Fighting Chance: The Story of the Sinking of Titanic.* North Mankato, MN: Capstone Press, 2016.

Sandler, Martin W. *The Whydah: A Pirate Ship Feared, Wrecked, and Found.* Somerville, MA: Candlewick Press, 2017.

Spilsbury, Richard. *Shipwrecked: Explore Floating and Sinking and Use Science to Survive.* Mankato, MN: Smart Apple Media/Black Rabbit Books, 2016.

Tougias, Michael J. and Casey Sherman. *The Finest Hours: The True Story of a Heroic Sea Rescue.* New York: Christy Ottaviano Books/Henry Holt and Company, 2014.

Index

About the Author

Joan Axelrod-Contrada is the author of 20 books for young people. She holds an MFA in writing for children and young adults from Vermont College of Fine Arts.